Office 2016 for Beginners
The Perfect Guide on Microsoft Office

Introduction

I want to thank you and congratulate you for downloading this book!

This book contains proven steps and strategies on how to learn using Microsoft office 2016. This book is easily written especially for beginners but other people can also be very benefited by reading this. I have written this book with basics, list, steps, shortcuts strategies, advices, tricks, techniques, steps, other valuable information so that you can easily understand the terms and quickly learn the using. This book is overall package of Microsoft office 2016 guide. So you can get the best guidance from this book about office 2016. So, download this book and get perfectly benefited.

Thanks again for downloading this book, I hope you enjoy it!

Chapter 1: What is Microsoft Office?

Microsoft Office is an arrangement of interrelated desktop applications, servers and administrations, aggregately alluded to as an office suite, for the Microsoft Windows and Mac OS X operating systems. This list contains every one of the programs that are, or have been, in Microsoft Office since it started and are in alphabetical order request.

Chapter 2: List of Microsoft Office Applications

Desktop applications

- ➢ Microsoft Access

- ➢ Microsoft Excel

- ➢ Microsoft OneNote

- ➢ Microsoft Outlook

- ➢ Microsoft PowerPoint

- ➢ Microsoft Project

- ➢ Microsoft Publisher

- ➢ Microsoft Visio

- ➢ Microsoft Word

- ➢ Skype for Business

Server applications

- ➢ Microsoft Exchange Server

- ➢ Outlook on the web

- ➢ Microsoft Project Server

- ➢ Office Web Apps Server

- ➢ SharePoint

- ➢ Excel Services

- ➢ InfoPath Forms Services

- ➢ Skype for Business Server

Online services

- ➢ Docs.com

- ➢ Office Online

- ➢ One Drive

- ➢ Outlook.com

- ➢ Sway

Discontinued programs

- ➢ Microsoft Binder

- ➢ Microsoft Clip Organizer

- ➢ Microsoft Data Analyzer

- ➢ Microsoft Entourage

- ➢ Microsoft Equation Editor

- ➢ Microsoft Exchange User

- ➢ Microsoft FrontPage

- ➢ Microsoft Graph

- ➢ Microsoft InfoPath

- ➢ Microsoft InterConnect

- Microsoft Mail

- Microsoft Office Accounting

- Microsoft Office Document Imaging

- Microsoft Office Document Scanning

- Microsoft Office Live

- Microsoft Office Live Meeting

- Microsoft Office PerformancePoint Server

- Microsoft Office Picture Manager

- Microsoft Office Project Portfolio Server

- Microsoft Outlook Hotmail Connector

- Microsoft PhotoDraw

- Microsoft Photo Editor

- Microsoft Schedule+

- Microsoft Search Server

- Microsoft SharePoint Designer

- Microsoft SharePoint Foundation

- Microsoft SharePoint Workspace

- Microsoft Vizact

- Office Assistant

- Office Web Components

- Ribbon Hero

- Ribbon Hero 2

Technologies

- Information Bridge

- Microsoft Office Open XML

- Microsoft Office XML formats

- Smart Tags

- Visual Basic for Applications

Chapter 3: What is new on Microsoft Office 2016?

Microsoft Office is a standout amongst the best items by Microsoft. It is accessible in the Windows and Apple's stages. Indeed, even it is also accessible in Android stage. Succeeding to giving the gigantic changes on the Microsoft Office 2013, Microsoft is developing the most recent form of the office application. And now, this is the Microsoft office 2016 user manual.

Overall, the new Microsoft Office will bring the comparable idea. It concentrates on productivity and shows up with the level and minimalist design. The new Microsoft Office is still most appropriate for PC with keyboard and mouse. And simply like the past adaptation, the user interface will be refreshing even there are some beautiful themes accessible.

In spite of the fact that there may be a few differences on the final rendition, you can get a few pictures from the designer review. Be that as it may, the best thing about Microsoft Office 2016 is about a single user experience. Users can get the same user experience and the same productivity in the mobile platform, for example, in Windows 10 for telephone and Windows 10 for desktop. Word and PowerPoint will be enhanced for mobile and touch also.

Esthetic department also changed. Smart scrolling and snap functions will make clicking spreadsheet to get less demanding. The new insight includes also bring the web references.

It just brings the new word reading knowledge. Interestingly, Microsoft Office 2016 will show up in two types. Microsoft Office for 8 inches devices or littler and for the bigger ones. Despite the fact that there are 2 flavors on the same Microsoft Office, the two of them will be worked with the same functionality. There also no differences on the other platforms, for example, Android, iOS or Windows.

The other new things about Microsoft Office 2016 are about the customizable theme. There is another beautiful theme on this form. So not at all like Microsoft Office 2013, office applications will show up with more colors. At any rate, each application will show up with its shading. If the past Microsoft Office Word just shows up with a little touch of blue shading and dominated by the white or the grey shading, the domination of the blue shading will develop on the new Microsoft Office Word. It stills keeping the utilization of ribbon and overall, it seems to be comparable with the past adaptation.

On the Microsoft office 2016 user manual, there also a noteworthy redesign on the existing application. In the most recent adaptation, Microsoft changes the ability to insert pictures to the document. Presently, it will revise the introduction automatically.

Chapter 4: Use of Microsoft Office application

Excel- Excel is an electronic spreadsheet program that can be utilized for storing, organizing and manipulating information. A spreadsheet has various inherent components and tools, for example, functions, formulas, charts, and data analysis tools that make it simpler to work with a lot of data

PowerPoint - PowerPoint is utilized for creating presentations. The pages, or slides, in PowerPoint can contain pictures, vast texts, diagrams, sounds, and other items to make the presentation all the more entertaining and simpler to understand. Organization diagrams can be made PowerPoint.

Word - Microsoft Word, or Word as it is usually known, is a software application that permits the user to perform word processing. Word can be utilized to make documents, for example, letters, invitations, research papers, flyers, resumes, books.

Access - Access is a social database program. It is utilized to track, store, and provide details regarding a lot of data.

OneNote – OneNote is a note-taking and information-management program which permits the user to button thoughts and information in electronic structure, and then format, sort out, and share that information. Documents and/or Web material can be put away in full color, searchable format or as icons.

Project – Project is a software application that gives project management tools (plan, arrange, manage resources) to oversee projects to finish a specific objective. It permits users to understand and control project timetables and finances, to convey and show project information, and to sort out work and people to make beyond any doubt that projects are finished on calendar.

Publisher - Publisher is a desktop publishing program mainly used to outline quality documents, for example, flyers, business cards, bulletins, calendars, brochures and posters. Publisher's file format is not perfect to other desktop publishing applications, for example, Corel Draw, Illustrator and Photoshop.

SharePoint - SharePoint is a joint effort stage for Web services. It offers a simplified user experience for the sharing of web journals, wikis, analysis, document libraries, and shared task lists. It includes a community gathering for users to take part in and sort discussions, a micro blogging capability and enhanced seek capabilities, an e-discovery functionality, claims-based authentication, and backing for mobile user. The business intelligence tools included in SharePoint empower business users to sort out objectives and procedures and also make customized data models, reports and dashboards.

Visio – Visio is a diagramming tool that can make complex charts in an easy to use way. It can be utilized to visually convey both specialized and non-specialized representations of thoughts, procedures, ideas, structures, layouts, models, blueprints, and so on.

Lync – Lync is video conferencing, online meeting, application sharing and coordinated effort, and instant messaging software item. Its most ordinarily utilized application is Skype.

Standpoint – Outlook is an email customer and individual information manager.

Office 365 for business – Office 365 is a subscription based online office and software plus services suite that offers access to different services and software worked around the MS Office stage. Its administrations include email, social networking and cooperation, and cloud storage.

Chapter 5: Shortcuts of

MICROSOFT OFFICE

Microsoft Word is a word processing program that was first made open by Microsoft in the early 1980s. It permits users to type and control text in a graphic sphere that looks like a page of paper. Additional elements, for example, tables, pictures and propelled formatting give users more choices to redo their documents. Over the past three decades, there have been various overhauls and additions to Microsoft Word. Today it is a standout amongst the most generally utilized word processors accessible for Macs and PCs. It is often taught to understudies in schools and required as a feature of the essential PC necessities for some office occupations. In this aide, new users will learn the fundamental elements of Microsoft Word and how to utilize them.

Alignment – The alignment choices manage whether the left and right edges of the text in a document hold fast to the right side, left, focus or justified. Alignment can be set from the formatting toolbar at the highest point of the window or under by choosing "paragraph" under the Format menu.

Bullets/Numbering – When creating a list of text items, users can browse a few slug or numbering framework to include a little realistic symbol or arrangement of numbers before every item. To add shots or numbering to a progression of text, click on the corresponding buttons in the formatting toolbar or pick "bullets and numbering" from the Format menu.

Clipboard – The clipboard goes about as a type of capacity zone when a bit of text is briefly evacuated and stored for later use within the same session. Using the Cut or Copy commands will put the text in the clipboard. Click on "Clipboard" under the Edit menu to view any text that might be briefly stored in it.

Copy – Copying text basically implies making an imitation of any text that is right now selecting and saving it to the clipboard. Pressing the Control and C keys in Windows or Command and C on a Mac will copy the text. On the other hand, users can also choose the text and then click the "Copy" choice under the Edit menu or in the main toolbar.

Cut – Cutting text expels the text from the visible document and stores it in the clipboard. Control-X or Command-X is the keyboard shortcuts for the Cut capacity on Windows and Mac individually. The Cut capacity can also be found under the Edit menu or the toolbar.

Document – Each document in Microsoft Word is basically another file. Every document can be a few pages in length. Another document can be made by hitting Control-N or Command-N, or by choosing the "New Blank Document" alternative from the File menu or the standard toolbar.

Edit – The edit menu or toolbar in Microsoft Word permits users to perform essential editing capacities in their document, for example, copying, cutting and pasting. It also contains alternatives for the Undo and Find/Repribbon capacities.

Font- Font is a type of outline for text and ordinarily incorporates this pattern into every letter, number and icon found on a keyboard. Text styles can go from formal to unusual. Microsoft Word accompanies a progression of gave fonts and additional ones can also be downloaded if required. To change the textual style utilized as a part of a document, select the text and either clicks on the main Font menu, the Font drop-down menu in the formatting toolbar or hit Control-D or Command D.

Footer – The footer is the text that consistently shows up on every page of a document, at the base of every page. Footers typically include points of interest, for example, the page number, or an organization's name and contact subtle elements in formal documents. Include or edit a footer by choosing "Header and Footer" under the View menu.

Format – The Format menu (or toolbar) goes above and beyond than the Edit menu. Users can make stylistic changes by changing the look of the text itself, paragraphs, lists and more.

Header – The header is like footer with the exception of that it sits at the exceptionally top of every page in a document. Headers often contain page numbers, the document name or sub-titles within a document. The header can be edited by clicking on "Header and Footer" within the View menu.

Justify, left justified, right justified – Justification is a type of alignment for text in a word processor. Justify guarantees that both the left and right sides of the text in every section keep running in a straight line. Left justify makes just the left half of the text adjusted, while the right side remains battered. Right justified does the finish opposite, with just the right half of the text adjusted. Users can apply justification to their text by clicking on the selecting so as to correspond buttons in the formatting toolbar or selecting the text and clicking on "Paragraph" under the Format menu.

Open – The Open command opens an existing document in Microsoft Word. Command or Control in addition to O, or choosing "Open... "From the File menu will give a pop-up window to users to choose the document they wish to open.

Paste – The paste command takes any beforehand duplicated or cut text and lays it down within the document where the cursor is pointing. Control or Command in addition to V, or "Paste" from the Edit menu or standard toolbar will run the paste capacity.

Print – The print command first opens a window where users can specify parameters of the paper, printer and ink they wish to print with and it gives a sneak peak of what the physical print will resemble. Control or Command in addition to P, or clicking on "Print" in the File menu or standard toolbar gives users a chance to get to the print window.

Quick access tool bar – The fast get to toolbar is a little and moveable toolbar at the top of the document window. It for the most part contains buttons to save, undo, re-do and print. This toolbar can also be customized to include or remove other commands.

Ribbon – The Ribbon is a type of toolbar found in variants of Microsoft Office 2007. It contains graphic buttons for commands and comparative commands are shown in groups for simple access.

Save – The save command is a standout amongst the most vital ones. It saves the majority of the work done to date within a document. The save command empowers users to come back to the same document later and continue writing, editing or printing. Control or Command plus S, or clicking "Save" under the

File menu or standard toolbar will save the document. The "Save As" alternative is somewhat different; it permits users to save the document as a different form by adding a different file name.

Text – Text is any of the words and paragraphs that a user types within a document.

Standard tool bar – The standard tool bar is the line of icons at the top of the document. Each of these buttons is utilized for fundamental functions, for example, saving, opening or printing documents, among other commands.

Undo– The undo highlight monitors every command that a user issues while working on their document. Issuing the undo command permits the user to do a reversal one step and restore the document as it was before their most recent editing command. Identified with the Undo command is Redo, which gives the user a chance to redo the same formatting command again. Control or Command plus Z, or "undo" under the Edit menu is utilized to undo a command, while Control or Command in addition to Y or "Re-try" under Edit is to redo a command.

Chapter 6: Word 2016

Quick Access Toolbar

Keep favorite commands for all time visible.

Explore the ribbon

See what Word can do by clicking the ribbon tabs and exploring accessible tools.

Discover contextual commands

Select tables, pictures, or other objects in a document to uncover additional tabs.

Find whatever you require

Gaze upward Word commands, get Help, or hunt the Web.

Share your work with others

Invite other people to see and edit cloud-based documents.

Navigate with ease

Utilize the discretionary, resizable sidebar to oversee long or complex documents.

Format with the Mini Toolbar

Snap or right-click text and objects to rapidly format them set up.

Show or hide the ribbon

Click the pin symbol to keep the ribbon displayed, or shroud it again by clicking the arrow.

Status bar shortcuts

Click any status bar indicator to explore your document, view word count statistics, or check your spelling.

Change your view

Click the status bar buttons to switch between view options or utilize the zoom slider to magnify the page display to your liking.

Create something

Begin with a Blank document to motivate right to work. On the other hand save yourself a set of time by selecting and then customizing a format that takes after what you require. Click File > New, and then select or hunt down the format you need.

Stay connected

Need to take a shot at the go and crosswise over different devices? Click File > Account to sign in and access your current utilized files anywhere, on any device, through consistent integration between Office, One Drive, One Drive for Business, and SharePoint.

Find current files

Whether you just work with records put away on your PC's local hard drive or you roam across various cloud services, clicking File > Open takes you to your current utilized documents and any records that you might have pinned to your list.

Find out contextual tools

You can make contextual ribbon commands accessible by selecting important objects in your document. For instance, clicking within a table displays the Table Tools tab, which offers additional choices for the Design and Layout of your tables.

Impart your work to others

To invite others to see or edit your documents in the cloud, click the Share button in the upper right corner of the application window. In the Share pane that opens, you can get a sharing link or send invitations to the people you select.

Review and track changes

Whether you simply need to check spelling, hold your word number under control, or completely work together with other people, the Review tab divulges fundamental commands to track, discuss, and deal with the greater part of the progressions made to your documents.

See who else is typing

Co-authoring Word documents that are shared on One Drive or on a SharePoint site happens continuously, which implies you can without much of a stretch see where other creators are making changes in the same document that you're as of now working in.

Format documents with style

The Styles sheet lets you visually make, apply, and survey the formatting styles in your present document. To open it, click the Home tab, and then click the little arrow in the lower right corner of the Styles gallery.

Find whatever you require

Type a keyword or phrase into the Tell me what you need to do seek box on the ribbon to rapidly find the Word features and commands you're looking for, to discover Help content, or to get more information online.

Get other Quick Start Guides

Word 2016 is only one of the recently designed applications in Office 2016. To download free Quick Start Guides for any of the other new forms of your favorite applications, visit http://aka.ms/office-2016-guides.

Look up related information

With Smart Lookup, Word searches the Internet for significant information to define words, phrases and concepts. Search results shown on the assignment sheet can give helpful context to the thoughts you've outlined in your documents.

Chapter 7: Tips That Can Make Anyone a Microsoft Word Expert

Microsoft Office is a standout amongst the most majority office suites out there. It's utilized by businesses both extensive and small. There are versions for college students and for home use. It's accessible for both PC and Mac and word around the internet grapevine is that it'll in the end be made accessible for a few distributions of Linux. Despite the fact that a great many people use it, the vast majority don't use it to its maximum capacity. Here are amazing tips to make you superior at Microsoft Word.

1. See all the symbols in Microsoft Word

When you type spaces and hit the enter button, you don't see all that much yet that doesn't mean there isn't anything there. There are really images and characters everywhere on your Microsoft Word document and you may not know it. If you need to see every one of them, go to File, then Options, then Display, and select to Always Show These Formatting Marks on the Screen. You can also actuate Draft Mode to see what the first doesn't by going to the View menu and setting it to Draft View.

2. Master the paragraph

You would be surprised exactly what number ways you can format paragraph. You can indent the primary sentence or you can indent every other line with the exception of the principal line. What's more, the paragraph mark (shown above) is quite intense. It contains information on how every paragraph is formatted which can make them truly effective. If you copy an entire section with the paragraph mark, you wind up copying the formatting too. If you don't copy the imprint with the section, the paragraph will paste without formatting.

3. Expert segments

By using the different breaks in Microsoft Word, you can better sort out your documents. The most ideal approach to do this is using areas. You can get to the breaks menu on the Page Layout menu. Microsoft Office doesn't see pages to be you and I see them. They see areas. If you set your document up in segments, you can format every segment independently and give yourself much more control than you regularly would if everything were in one part!

4. Use styles

Styles are amazingly capable. If you make a style layout, you can utilize it over and over again for any document. If you write a ton of reminders, you can make an update style. You can rehash the procedure for all intents and purposes any document type. To see existing styles, to the Home tab in Word. You can click on the down arrow to make your own. If you write a great deal in a comparative style, it's definitely worth turning it into a style so you don't need to format so much and save yourself some time.

5. Set up your document before writing

It's generally a good idea to think about your formatting before you really begin filling in the spaces. That way you can format your headers, paragraphs, styles, and so on all before you set up your document together. Doing so can permit you to modify your document before you make it to ensure beyond any doubt that everything fits properly. There's nothing more frustrating than copying and pasting some information and having the formatting all off-base.

6. Configure your paste choices

Trust it or not, you can really control how Microsoft Office manages pasting words. This can be attained by clicking on the Office button (the logo at the upper left), navigating to Word Options, and then to Advanced. From there you ought to have the capacity to see a Cut, Copy, and Paste choice that will give you a chance to configure your option. This can permit you to do things like disable hyper linking while pasting and other formatting alternatives to make life simpler.

7. Utilize full justification formatting

An often obscure choice in Word is the ability to utilize justification formatting. You can see an illustration of this above. Basically, it just implies that the left and right margins are perfectly adjusted. Word is ready to do this by altering the spacing of words in every line with the goal that they line up. This gives documents a professional and formal look. To utilize this, click the Office logo, then Word Options, and then Advanced. Expand the Layout Options and you can set it there.

8. Conceal the ribbon interface

For the individuals who may not know, the ribbon interface is the toolbar that keeps running along the top of Microsoft Word. A few people appreciate it and others find it distracting and too occupied. Thankfully, there is a simple approach to dispose of the strip. With Word open, click CTRL+F1. The ribbon will disappear. Rehash the procedure to make it return.

10. Evacuate all formatting

Now and then you have to explode the formatting and begin once again. Formatting can get disorganized and your document can wind up looking terrible. At the point when this happens it's presumably best to begin once again from the beginning. To do this, select any bit of text you need to expel the formatting from and click the button as shown in the screenshot above. The formatting will be removed and you will be left with just text.

11. Utilize the Spike to copy and paste

Spike pasting is really a great deal of fun. Here's the premise. You cut different words from a document and then you can paste them all together. There isn't generally a specific use-case for this tool yet you'll know when you require it. To utilize it, use CTRL+F3 to copy. You can do this the same number of times as you like. When you paste of course, it'll paste everything that you duplicated using the CTRL+F3 command. This can be valuable for collecting pieces of a document and putting them together.

With these tricks and a little practice, you'll have the capacity to make amazing documents that'll look professional and clean. In a word place where simply knowing how to utilize Word isn't sufficient any longer, these tips can give you a slight edge that'll make you stand out!

Chapter 8: Excel 2016

Snappy Access Toolbar

Keep favorite commands forever visible.

Explore the ribbon

See what Excel can do by clicking the ribbon tabs and exploring accessible tools.

Discover contextual commands

Select tables, charts, or other items in a word book to uncover additional tabs.

Find whatever you require

Turn upward Excel commands; get Help, or search the Web.

Impart your work to others

Invite other people to see and edit cloud-based wordbooks

Insert and edit functions

Utilize the formula bar to view or edit the chose cell or to insert functions into your formulas.

Customized charts

Select a graph to quickly add, change, or uproot any existing chart, elements and formatting.

Show or conceal the ribbon

Click the pin symbol to keep the ribbon displayed, or conceal it again by clicking the arrow.

Switch or make sheets

Click the sheet tabs to switch between work book sheets or to make new ones.

Change your view

Click the status bar buttons to switch between view choices, or utilize the zoom slider to magnify the sheet display to your liking.

Create something

Begin with a Blank word book to inspire right to work. Alternately save yourself a bundle of time by selecting and then customizing a format that looks like what you require. Click File > New, and then select or hunt down the layout you need.

Stay associated

Need to deal with the go and crosswise over different devices? Click File > Account to sign in and access your current used anywhere, on any device, through consistent integration between Office, OneDrive, OneDrive for Business, and SharePoint.

Find current files

Whether you just work with records put away on your PC's local hard drive or you wander crosswise over different cloud devices, clicking File > Open takes you to your currently used wordbooks and any documents that you might have pinned to your list.

Discover contextual tools

Select important objects in your wordbook to make contextual commands accessible. For instance, clicking a chart element displays the Chart Tools tab with alternatives for the Design and Format of a selected chart

Share your work to others

To invite others to see or edit your wordbooks in the cloud, click the Share button in the upper right corner of the application window. In the Share sheet that opens, you can get a sharing link or send invitations to the people you select.

Manage data with Excel tables

You can format any scope of cells in your present wordbook as an Excel table. Excel tables let you investigate and effectively deal with a gathering of related information independently from the other lines and paragraphs in your wordbook

Insert functions, create formulas

On the Formulas tab, click Insert Function to display the Insert Function dialog box. Here, you can search for and insert functions, turn upward the correct syntax, and even get top to bottom Help about how your chose functions work.

Find whatever you require

Type a keyword or phrase into the Tell me what you need to do seek box on the ribbon to rapidly find the Excel features and commands you're looking for, to discover Help content, or to get more information online.

Get other Quick Start Guides

Excel2016 is only one of the recently designed applications in Office 2016. To download free Quick Start Guides for any of the other new forms of your favorite applications, visit http://aka.ms/office-2016-guides.

Look up important information

With Smart Lookup, Excel hunts the Internet down pertinent information to define words, phase and concepts. List items shown on the task pane can give helpful context to the data and information in your wordbooks.

Chapter 9: How to Use Excel

If you experience a situation where you have to physically upgrade your information, you're likely missing out on an equation that can do it for you. Before spending a really long time counting cells or coping and pasting information, search for a speedy fix on Excel - you'll likely find one.

In the spirit of working all the more proficiently and avoiding monotonous, manual work, here are a couple Excel traps to kick you off with how to utilize Excel.

How to Use Excel

1) Pivot Tables

Turn Tables are utilized to rearrange information in a spreadsheet. They won't change the information that you have, however they can whole up qualities and look at different information in your spreadsheet, depending on what you'd like them to do.

How about we examine a case. Suppose I need to investigate what number people are in every house at Hogwarts. You might be thinking that I don't have too much information, however for more information sets; this will prove to be useful.

To make the Pivot Table, I go to Data > Pivot Table. Excel will consequently populate your Pivot Table, yet you can simply change around the request of the information. Then, you have four choices to look over.

1.   Report Filter: This permits you to just take a gander at certain columns in your dataset. For instance, if I needed to make a channel by house, I could decide to just include understudies in Gryffindor instead of all understudies.

2.   Column Labels: These could be your headers in the dataset.

3.   Row Labels: These could be your columns in the dataset. Both Row and Column names can contain information from your segments (e.g. to start with Name can be dragged to either the Row or Column name - it just relies on upon how you need to see the information.)

4.   Value: This segment permits you to take a gander at your information differently.

Instead of simply pulling in any numeric worth, you can whole, check, normal, max, min, tally numbers, or do a couple of other controls with your information. Truth is told, by default, when you drag a field to Value, it generally does a number.

Since I need to include the quantity of understudies every house, I'll go to the Pivot Table and drag the House section to both the Row Labels and the Values. This will aggregate up the quantity of understudies connected with every house.

2) Add More Than One New Row or Column

As you play around with your information, you may find you're continually needing to include more lines and segments. Once in a while, you might even need to include many columns. Doing this one-by-one would be super dull. Fortunately, there's dependably a less demanding way.

To include various lines or segments in a spreadsheet, highlight the same number of preexisting lines or segments that you need to include. Then, right-click and select "Insert."

In the illustration beneath, I need to add an additional three lines. By highlighting three lines and then clicking insert, I'm ready to add an additional three clear columns into my spreadsheet rapidly and effortlessly.

3) Filters

When you're looking at substantial information sets, you don't typically should be looking at every single column in the meantime. Some of the time, you just need to take a gander at information that fit into certain criteria. That is where channels come in.

Channels permit you to pare down your information to just take a gander at certain lines at one time. In Excel, a channel can be added to every section in your information - and from there, you can then pick which cells you need to see on the double.

How about we investigate the case underneath. Include a channel by clicking the Data tab and selecting "Channel." Clicking the arrow alongside the segment headers and you'll have the capacity to pick whether you need your information to be organizing in ascending or descending request, and in addition which specific lines you need to show.

In my Harry Potter sample, suppose I just need to see the understudies in Gryffindor. By selecting the Gryffindor channel, the other columns disappear.

Star Tip: Copy and paste the qualities in the spreadsheet when a Filter is on to do additional analysis in another spreadsheet.

4) Remove Duplicates

Bigger information sets have a tendency to have copy content. You might have a list of different contacts in an organization and just need to see the quantity of organizations you have. In situations like this, removing the copies comes in quite handy.

To uproot your copies, highlight the line or segment that you need to evacuate copies of. Then, go to the Data tab, and select "Evacuate

Duplicates" (under Tools). A pop-up will seem to affirm which information you need to work with. Select "Evacuate Duplicates and you're ready.

You can also utilize this element to uproot a whole line in light of copy section esteem. So if you have three lines with Harry Potter's information and you just need to see one, then you can choose the entire dataset and then evacuate copies taking into account email. You're resulting list will have just interesting names without any copies.

5) Transpose

When you have low lines of information in your spreadsheet, you may choose you really need to change the items in one of those lines into paragraphs (or the other way around). It would require a great deal of investment to copy and paste every individual header - yet what the transpose highlight permits you to do is just move your line information into paragraphs, or the other route around.

Begin by highlighting the segment that you need to transpose into columns. Right-click it, and then select "Copy." Next, select the cells on your spreadsheet where you need your first line or segment to begin. Right-click on the cell, and then select "Paste Special." A module will show up - at the base, you'll see a choice to transpose. Watch that container and select OK. Your segment will now be exchanged to a line or vise versa.

6) Text to Columns

What if you need to split out information that is in one cell into two different cells? For instance, possibly you need to haul out somebody's organization name through their email address. Alternately maybe you need to partitioned somebody's full name into a first and last name for your email marketing formats.

Because of Excel, both are conceivable. In the first ribbon, highlight the section that you need to split up. Next, go to the Data tab and select "Text to Columns." A module will show up with additional information.

To start with, you have to choose either "Delimited" or "Settled Width."

- "Delimited" implies you need to separate the segment in view of characters, for example, commas, spaces, or tabs.

- "Fixed Width" implies you need to choose the definite area on every one of the segments that you need the split to happen.

In the sample case beneath, how about we select "Delimited" so we can isolate the full name into first name and last name.

Then, it's a great opportunity to pick the Delimiters. This could be a tab, semi-colon, comma, space, or something else. ("Something else" could be the "@" sign utilized as a part of an email address, for instance.) In our illustration, how about we pick the space. Excel will then show you a review of what your new paragraphs will resemble.

When you're content with the sneak peak, press "Next." This page will permit you to choose Advanced formats if you decide to. When you're set, click "Finish."

7) Simple Calculations

In addition to doing entirely complex estimations, Excel can offer you some assistance with doing straightforward arithmetic like adding, subtracting, multiplying, or dividing any of your information.

- To include, utilize the + sign.

- To subtract, utilize the - sign.

- To increase, utilize the * sign.

- To separate, utilize the/sign.

You can also utilize parenthesis to guarantee certain figuring's are done first. In the case beneath (10+10*10), the second and third 10 were multiplied together before adding the additional 10. However, if we made it (10+10)*10, the first and second 10 would be included first.

Reward: If you need the normal of an arrangement of numbers, you can utilize the formula=AVERAGE (Cell Range). If you need to aggregate up a segment of numbers, you can utilize the equation =SUM (Cell Range).

8) Conditional Formatting Formula

Conditional formatting permits you to change a cell's shading in view of the information within the cell. For instance, if you need to hail certain numbers that are above normal or in the main 10% of the information in your spreadsheet, you can do that. If you need to shading code commonalities between different lines in Excel, you can do that. This will help you rapidly see information the is vital to you.

To begin, highlight the gathering of cells you need to utilize conditional formatting on. Then, pick "Conditional Formatting" from the Home menu and select your rationale from the dropdown. (You can also make your own particular standard if you need something different.) A window will appear that prompts you to give more information about your formatting guideline. Select "alright" when you're set and you ought to see your outcomes consequently show up.

9) IF Statement

Once in a while, we would prefer not to tally the quantity of times a worth shows up. Instead, we need to input different information into a cell if there is a corresponding cell with that information.

For instance, in the situation beneath, I need to honor ten points to everyone who has a ribbon in the Gryffindor house. Instead of physically typing in 10's alongside each Gryffindor understudy's name, I can utilize the IF THEN Excel equation to say that if the understudy is in Gryffindor, then they ought to get ten points.

The equation: IF (logical_test, value_if_true, estimation of false)

Sample Shown Below: =IF (D2="Gryffindor","10","0")

When all is said in done terms, the equation would be IF (Logical Test, estimation of genuine, estimation of false). How about we delve into each of these variables.

- Logical_Test: The legitimate test is the "IF" part of the announcement. For this situation, the rationale is D2="Gryffindor" in light of the fact that we need to make beyond any doubt that the cell corresponding with the understudy says "Gryffindor." Make beyond any doubt to ribbon Gryffindor in quotes here.

- Value_if_True: This is what we need the cell to show if the worth is valid. For this situation, we need the cell to show "10" to indicate that the understudy was recompensed the 10 points. Just utilize quotes if you need the outcome to be text instead of a number.

- Value_if_False: This is what we need the cell to show if the worth is false. For this situation, for any understudy not in Gryffindor, we need the cell to show "0" to show 0 points. Just utilize quotes if you need the outcome to be text instead of a number.

10) Dollar Signs

Have you ever seen a dollar sign in an Excel equation? At the point when utilized as a part of an equation, it isn't representing an American dollar; instead, it makes beyond any doubt that the definite segment and column are held the same regardless of the fact that you copy the same recipe in contiguous lines.

A cell reference - when you allude to cell A5 from cell C5, for instance - is relative as a matter of course. All things considered, you're really referring to a phone that is five segments to one side (C minus an) and in the same column (5). This is known as a relative equation. When you copy a relative equation from one cell to another, it'll conform the qualities in the recipe taking into account where it's moved. In any case, some of the time, we need those qualities to continue through to the end regardless of whether they're moved around or not - and we can do that by making the recipe in the phone into what's called an outright equation.

To change the relative recipe (=A5+C5) into an outright equation, we'd go before the line and section values by dollar signs, similar to this: (=$A$5+$C$5).

Chapter 10: PowerPoint 2016

Fast Access Toolbar

Keep favorite commands for all time visible.

Investigate the strip

See what PowerPoint can do by clicking the strip tabs and exploring accessible tools.

Discover contextual commands

Select text, pictures, or other items in a presentation to uncover additional tabs.

Find whatever you require

Gaze upward PowerPoint commands, get Help, or hunt the Web.

Impart your work to others

Invite other people to see and edit cloud-based presentations.

Explore and sort out

Click a slide thumbnail to switch to it or drag a slide to move it up or down in the list.

Show or shroud the strip

Click the pin symbol to keep the strip displayed, or shroud it again by clicking the arrow.

Pivot objects set up

Openly control the position of text boxes, pictures, and other chose objects.

Begin the show

Click here to display from the present slide, or click the Slide Show tab on the ribbon.

Change your perspective

Click the status bar buttons to switch between perspectives, or utilize the zoom slider to magnify the slide display to your liking.

Make something

Begin with a Blank Presentation to motivate right to work. On the other hand save yourself a group of time by selecting and then customizing a layout that looks like what you require. Click File > New, and then select or look for the format you need.

Stay associated

Need to deal with the go and crosswise over different devices? Click File > Account to sign in and access you're as of late utilized records anywhere, on any device, through consistent integration between Office, OneDrive, OneDrive for Business, and SharePoint.

Find late documents

Whether you just work with documents put away on your PC's nearby hard drive or you meander crosswise over different cloud administrations, clicking File > Open takes you to your as of late utilized presentations and any records that you might have pinned to your list.

Impart your work to others

To invite others to see or edit your presentations in the cloud, click the Share button in the upper right corner of the application window. In the Share sheet that opens, you can get a sharing link or send invitations to the people you select.

Get inspired while you work

In a hurry or feeling uninspired? Let PowerPoint make awesome looking slides

For you in light of the substance you've included. Insert or paste a picture on your present slide and then snap your favored format in the Design Ideas assignment sheet.

Format shapes with precision

Precisely format a chose picture, shape, or protest with the extensive tools accessible in the Format Shape errand sheet. To display it, click the Home tab, and then click the little arrow in the lower right corner of the Drawing strip bunch.

Transform pictures and protests

PowerPoint 2016 introduces Morph, another cinematic impact that makes smooth, energized transitions by tracking and moving pictures and other objects over numerous slides in your presentation.

Make another slide and then include any text and pictures or questions that you need. This first slide indicates the position of objects toward the beginning of the transition.

Next, right-click the slide thumbnail and snap Duplicate Slide.

On the replicated slide, move and resize any of the text, pictures, or questions as required. For instance, you can make an item stand out by increasing its size, or you can line things up and include portrayals. This second slide indicates the situation of objects toward the end of the transition.

To apply the impact, select both slide thumbnails, click the Transitions ribbon tab, and then snap Morph. PowerPoint tracks the objects found on both slides and then vivify their size and position when the impact is seen.

To see the impact, click Preview on the Transitions ribbon tab. If you need to tweak the impact, click the Effect Options button on the Transitions tab.

Find whatever you require

Type a keyword or expression into the Tell me what you need to do seek box on the strip to rapidly find the PowerPoint components and commands you're looking for, to discover Help content, or to get more information online.

Get other Quick Start Guides

PowerPoint 2016 is only one of the recently outlined applications in Office 2016. To download our free Quick Start Guides for any of the other new forms of your favorite applications, visit http://aka.ms/office-2016-guides.

Turn upward important information

With Smart Lookup, PowerPoint scans the Internet for important information to define words, expressions, and ideas. Indexed lists shown on the errand sheet can give helpful context to the thoughts you're sharing in your presentations.

Chapter 11: PowerPoint Basics

Microsoft's PowerPoint is an intense presentation tool with which you can make professional slide shows. The following tips are my favorites for understudies in my online classes. For significantly more tips about PowerPoint, visit Microsoft's Office Web site: http://www.microsoft.com/office/powerpoint or scan the Web for +PowerPoint +tips. To peruse an interesting article about PowerPoint, look at the following Web site: http://www.teach-nology.com/instructional exercises/PowerPoint/

The tips underneath are partitioned into four classes: Tips 1-7 are fundamental PowerPoint tips for beginners. Tips 8-14 are tips for more progressed PowerPoint users. Tips 15-25 are tips to work with illustrations. Finally, four additional tips have been included for when you are presenting your slide show in individual.

1. Fundamental Rules and Configuration

Utilize the PowerPoint Light Bulb to guide slide-show mechanics; make certain no lights are remaining on any slides. To set the "light bulbs" to favored settings, go into the Tools > Options > Spelling and Style tab. Make certain the checkbox for "Check Style" is stamped then click the "Style Options" button. Set the design for the following:

Case and End Punctuation tab:

- Slide title style: Title Case

- Slide title punctuation (no mark in this checkbox)
- Body text style: Sentence Case
- Body punctuation: Paragraphs have consistent punctuation

Visual Clarity tab:

- Number of fonts should not exceed **3**
- Number of lines should not exceed **6**
- Title text size should be at least **36**
- Body text size should be at least **20**
- Number of lines per title should not exceed **2**
- Number of lines per bullet should not exceed **2**

Then make certain your light bulb is turned on:

In the Help menu, turn on the Office Assistant.

As you are creating a slide, the light bulb might show up. If it appears, you are breaking a standard for good slide show mechanics. Click on the light bulb to see the mistake. In numerous cases PowerPoint will alter the mistake for you if you permit it. When I score (grade) your PowerPoint slide show, I will deduct one mechanics point for every light bulb remaining in your show.

2. The Mighty Shift Key

> ➢ Hold down the SHIFT key when drawing an oval to get a perfectly round circle.
>
> ➢ Hold down the SHIFT key when drawing a line to get a perfectly straight line.
>
> ➢ Hold down the SHIFT key while clicking on the normal view icon to get the Master slide.

- Hold down the SHIFT key while clicking on the slide sorter view to get the handouts master.
- Hold down the SHIFT key while resizing a graphic to retain the same proportions in the resized graphic.
- Hold down the SHIFT key when drawing a rectangle to get a square.
- Hold down the SHIFT key while pressing Enter to get a blank line without a bullet.
- Hold down the SHIFT key while pressing F3 to change the case of letters.
- Hold down the SHIFT key to select multiple objects on a slide at the same time.

3. The Mighty Control Key

- ➢ Hold down the CTRL key while turning the wheel on the mouse to zoom in and out of the slide
- ➢ Hold down the CTRL key plus the HOME key to go to the first slide
- ➢ Hold down the CTRL key plus the END key to go to the last slide in your presentation
- ➢ Hold down the CTRL key while clicking the slide show view button when you are editing a slide show. This will open a preview window so you can see that slide in slide show mode.
- ➢ Hold down the CTRL key while dragging an existing Guide to create a new guide.
- ➢ CTRL + A (in slide sorter view) to select all slides

- CTRL + A (on the Slides tab) to select all objects
- CTRL + A (on the Outline tab) to select all text in your slide show
- CTRL + B to apply bold formatting
- CTRL + C to copy the selected object
- CTRL + D to duplicate (make a copy of) the selected slide
- CTRL + E to center a paragraph
- CTRL + F to find text
- CTRL + G to open the grids and guidelines dialog box
- CTRL + H to replace text
- CTRL + I to apply italic formatting
- CTRL + J to justify a paragraph (full alignment)
- CTRL + K to insert a hyperlink
- CTRL + L to left align a paragraph

- CTRL + M to insert a new slide
- CTRL + N to create a new presentation
- CTRL + O to open an existing presentation
- CTRL + P to print a presentation
- CTRL + Q to quit PowerPoint
- CTRL + R to right align a paragraph
- CTRL + S to save a presentation
- CTRL + T to change the formatting of characters between sentence, lowercase, and uppercase
- CTRL + U to apply underline formatting
- CTRL + V to paste a cut or copied object
- CTRL + W to close a presentation
- CTRL + X to cut a selected objected
- CTRL + Y to redo or repeat an action
- CTRL + Z to undo the last action

- ➢ CTRL + Equal Sign to apply subscript formatting
- ➢ CTRL + SHIFT + Plus Sign to apply superscript formatting
- ➢ CTRL + Space Bar to remove subscript and superscript

5. Inserting Special Symbols

- ➢ To insert the copyright © symbol, enter (c)
- ➢ To insert the Trademark ™ symbol enter (tm)
- ➢ To insert the registered ® symbol enter (r)
- ➢ You can make your own special symbol shortcuts in Tools > AutoCorrect (copy from character map and paste into replace with)

6. Maintain a strategic distance from Beginner's Mistakes

> Use traditional shading conspires that has been turned out to be simple on the eyes. Keep in mind that the information in your slide show is more vital than the colors. Information, not showy colors, ought to draw in your viewers' consideration.

> Limit the utilization of movements. Over the top liveliness will distract your viewers' from the information in your slide show. If you utilize movements, utilize the same types of activities on all slides- - a professional slide show is not an ideal opportunity to perceive what number different liveliness you can utilize.

➤ Limit the transitions between slides. If you utilize a transition, utilize the same transition between all slides. A professional slide show is not an ideal opportunity to check whether you can utilize a different transition between every slide.

➤ Keep the slide show short, straightforward, and sweet. Focus on the message of the presentation rather than on the glitz accessible in PowerPoint.

➤ Create a title slide and at THE END slide in your presentation. Also, make a CREDITS slide if you utilize information or illustrations other than clasp workmanship furnished with PowerPoint. Using information or design without citing your source is considered plagiarism.

➢ Don't utilize various foundations. A professional slide show will be consistent.

➢ Don't utilize over the top representation and text impacts. A professional slide show will be inconspicuous and won't take away from the message.

➢ Use sound and moving illustrations just if the message of the presentation will be upgraded by it.

8. Editing Shortcuts

While selecting an item (a text pribbonholder or a graphical article), utilize the right mouse button to click on it (with Macintosh, use CTRL + click). Will you choose the item as well as you will be shown an editing menu specific to that protest?

9. Diminish File Size

Keep in mind that every slide in a PowerPoint presentation takes around 1-2 minutes to discuss. In that capacity, keep the quantity of slides in your presentation to a minimum. If you have a 15-minute presentation, set up close to 10-12 slides. Keep in mind, your oral presentation will require significant investment and you will need to save time for your group of onlookers to make inquiries. If your presentation is formal to the point that your gathering of people doesn't feel good to make inquiries, the presentation won't satisfy its intended mission. In addition, it is ideal to have your presentation take five minutes not exactly the dispensed time rather than to go one minute over.

If you need to decrease the span of the slide show record (on the grounds that your PC's memory is limited or for saving to a blaze drive or for transferring by means of email or the Internet), you can do four things:

•   Use Save As (in the File menu) and save your record using a different name.

•   Insert a clear slide toward the begin of your presentation.

•   If you are using the same realistic on a few slides, don't insert the realistic on each of the slides. Insert it just once, and then copy it from slide to slide. If you are using the same realistic on ALL slides, put the realistic on the expert slide (in the View menu.

• Look again at every realistic and other objects in your presentation. Do they add to the presentation or are they essentially "window dressing?" Consider simplifying so as to reduce the span of the slide show the additional impacts. Keep in mind: the information on your slides ought not to be overshadowed by the representation and embellishments.

10. Tearing off Sub-menus

You might need to utilize the same sub-menu a few times. If the sub-menu has a shaded bar at the top, you can "remove it" and spot it on the screen (see red arrow on realistic to one side). Simply drag the sub-menu with the mouse by that shaded bar.

11. Consistent Screen Builds

If you are creating a final slide where every article will be included dynamic slides, you can utilize a "retrogressive" trap to make your consistent screen construct. Make the final slide first. Then copy that slide (CTRL + D) the same number of times as important to fabricate the grouping. Then working in reverse, evacuate the items on the slides. This will guarantee that every article is in precisely the correct spot on every slide, and this eliminates those unattractive shifts when moving between slides.

12. Recycling Slides

It is conceivable to import a single slide or a gathering of slides from another presentation into your new presentation. If you have invested energy creating the perfect slide with a quote, unique realistic, or intricate graph on a slide, you can insert that slide into your new presentation (utilize the Insert > Slides from Files). Truth be told, you can insert slides from various presentations into your new presentation. Just the objects from the foreign made slides are inserted; the foundation and expert slide are unaffected.

13. A Summary Slide

With PowerPoint, you can rapidly add a Summary Slide to your presentation. This Summary Slide can be put at the first of your presentation as an introduction, or it can be moved to the end of your presentation as a conclusion or survey slide. The outline slide is made from the titles of the other slides:

1.   On the View menu, click Slide Sorter.

2. Select the slides with the titles you need to utilize. To choose numerous slides, hold down CTRL and snap the slides you need. (Make sure to choose the slides that will best compress your presentation.)

3. On the Slide Sorter toolbar, click the Summary Slide button.

4. A new slide, titled "Rundown Slide," shows up before the initially chose slide.

5. Edit this slide and/or move it to the fancied area in your slide show.

14. Install a Presentation in Word

To insert your slide show into a Word document, open both records (the slide show presentation in PowerPoint and the wanted document in Word):

1.   On the View menu, click Slide Sorter.

2.   Select the slides you need to utilize. To choose different slides, hold down CTRL and snap the slides you need.

3.   Copy the slides and paste them into Word (CTRL-C in PowerPoint and CTRL-V in Word).

You'll just see the primary slide in your Word document; however you can double click on that first slide to run the slide show.

Conclusion

Thank you again for getting this book!

I hope this book was able to help you to learn using Microsoft office 2016. Hope you got your desired information and tricks to use it. The next step is to implement the ideas on your practical life. Hope you'll be very successful in that platform.

Finally, if you enjoyed the book, then I'd like to ask you for a favor, would you be kind enough to leave a review for this book on Amazon? It'd be greatly appreciated!

Thank you and good luck!